John Miller's powerful and captivating collection begins *in media res*, at his father's deathbed, and broadens to encompass a series of carefully observed and fiercely imagined laments—for his brilliant and intimidating progenitor, but also for others important in the author's life, for the watery terrain and hurricane lilies of his youth on the Gulf Coast, and—far from least—for the historical and present harms done to America's most vulnerable. "The past is a prison the South is afraid to leave," writes Miller, but vigorous and incisive remembrance, as embodied in these poems, has the power to open that locked cell and force its ghosts into the open. "Ours the privilege to buoy memories / of those who came before / into futures we cannot know." These are poems of grief—they point to hope.

—Joel Brouwer
professor of English, University of Alabama

The mud flats, magnolias, and thunderheads of this collection evoke the Mobile delta with such perfection that readers will feel themselves in the humidity of a Southern night with the lapping of the tides as background music. Amid this poetic precision, Miller asks us to peel back layers of grief and family history to examine the multitude of stories, people, and places that make us who we are. Each line blooms with appreciation of the life that persists even in the face of loss.

—Jessica Fordham Kidd
author of *Bad Jamie*

"Grief stems from the same root / as gravity," John Miller reminds us in this incredible new book. *How My Father*

Became a Boat is a collection of poems that reminds me of the doxologies of loss, a collection that "keep[s] the sacraments of language." And it's this sacramental language that dots the crest of each wave off some humid southern shore, finding the knotted clews of our shared grammars uttered about a deathbed where "loss is not a cleaving to / but a cleaving from." Silences and absences fill each bright page here as Miller gives all of us a new elegy, a new "search for mirages that speak presence / but mean absence." That is, he reminds us in the blank black, "how we find / the isn't that is."

—MATTHEW MINICUCCI
winner of the Stafford/Hall Oregon Book Award

In this rich Southern collection of poems, the timeless and universal grief of a father's death serves as the backdrop for more specific twenty-first century griefs such as police brutality, climate change, and a global pandemic. Balancing elegy and ode, *How My Father Became a Boat* compassionately explores the complex experience of living in Alabama. Rhythmic and musical, Miller's words become a body of water, and the reader becomes a boat rocking back and forth on each verse. "What's a river?" the speaker's three-year-old nephew asks in the titular poem, and indeed, only by reading the entire book does the reader find the answer to that profound question.

—SARA PIRKLE
author of *The Disappearing Act*

For those of us who have tried to use language to describe the unfathomable wake a life leaves behind it—particularly a father's life—this book will give us hope.

It can, indeed, be articulated. All of it. In John Miller's beautiful new book, *How my Father Became a Boat*, grief's complications—its "symmetries" and contradictions—are explored with incredible maturity, generosity, and even humor. I will keep re-reading this book as I keep trying to understand why, when we grieve, we always seem to "grieve anew."

—Lauren Slaughter
author of *Spectacle*

These aching portraits are word made flesh, word made clay, made coastline. My kind of holy. Miller saves us with his syllables. Just as Phil Levine did. And Brad Watson did. And Jane Kenyon. And I am held above grief's waters by Miller's injustice songs: his keen-eyed scythe gleaning reds redder than the clay, threshing the ghosts. Friends, so much lasts in the shaky calm after the final page. I see the pelican's shadow turning in the scotch's amends. Hear the curl of the wave of the heart. Sense how a poem might well be a necktie: loose and tight; that stretch of road between song's throat and the heart's salty bay.

—Abraham Smith
author of *Insomniac Sentinel* and *Dear Weirdo*

"Bless Her Heart," the title of the first poem in John Miller's extraordinary elegiac collection, *How My Father Became a Boat*, and a Southern idiomatic expression indicative of ankle-nipping "Alabama Nice" for the naïve or ignorant, introduces the reader to a father under hospice care and a nurse's well-meaning but unwanted platitudes about death. The father hilariously responds LO—QUA—CIOUS, which provokes "exhausted laughter" for the family to carry with them during a time of grief and provides us with insight into the father and his relationship with his family in one physically labored, highfalutin word. This tenderness and biting wit, along with the conceit of the father as a boat and the Tensaw Delta and Mobile Bay—waterways that spark the imagination and memory—as the path to emotional healing become an amazing vehicle for loss and solace in the poems, which could easily fall into a heavy-handed cliché. Instead, Miller does not approach the natural world "with expectation," stamping revelations and coy insight as Thoreau in "Higher Laws" says philosophers and poets do too often. The speaker humbly reads the tides and their nuances, a skill that anyone navigating a delta would have to study; he shows us the tide lines where specks and reds stack up to feed on finger mullet and glass minnows and rigs fenders on boats and ties half-hitches and dedicates poems to things as seemingly mundane as ballasts and keels. All this acumen comes from the father, the Old Salt and hard-nosed lawyer, and reliving these experiences and laboring, hands tying knots and navigating oyster crags and widowmakers at low tide and luring Spanish Mackerel once he has passed, transforms to touching reunions with him. This collection places Miller among the best Southern poets writing today.

—ADAM VINES

author of *Lures*, editor of *Birmingham Poetry Review*

How My Father Became a Boat

John Miller

Fernwood
PRESS

How My Father Became a Boat
©2025 by John Miller

Fernwood Press
Newberg, Oregon
www.fernwoodpress.com

All rights reserved. No part may be reproduced
for any commercial purpose by any method without
permission in writing from the copyright holder.

Printed in the United States of America

Cover and page design: Eric Muhr
Cover art: Mikael Stenberg via Unsplash

ISBN 978-1-59498-169-2

for my father

Contents

OED 15
    Bless Her Heart 16
    Cleaving 17
    After a Prolonged Illness 18
    Panic Attack with Grief and Clavier 20
    The Funeral Director's Eyes 21
    OED 22
    Lessons in the Hidden Tongue 23
    His Sky-Blue Tie 24
    How My Father Became a Boat 25
Calculations from the Moral Arc 27
    Where Does a River End? 28
    Hurricane Lilies 29
    Calculations from the Moral Arc 30
    The Lesson 32
    Backroads Ovid 33
    Sleeping Porch 34
    Evinrude Ode 35
    Recipe with Healthy Crime 36
    Of Time and Tide 39
A Ripple of Hope 41
    A Ripple of Hope 42

  Greatest of These 43
  Eye of the Storm 44
  Consulting the Book of Rumination 46
  Plague Summer, College Town 48
  Be it Ever So Humble 49
  Where's Your Accent? 50
  Heat Lightning 51
Ebb Tide 53
  Elegy for Hustle-man 54
  Ship-breaking 55
  Hope's Hollow Bones 57
  Memorial Day 59
  Elegy with Black Holes and Hawking Radiation 60
  Tidewater Hedge-Witch 61
  What the Dead Want 64
  Ebb Tide 65
Keeping the Sacraments 67
  My Drug of Choice Is the Dictionary 68
  How to Speak with Ghosts 70
  Keeping the Sacraments 71
  Memory's Edges 72
  The Sacrament of Solitude 74
  The Benediction 75
  Vessels 76
Reading the Gulf 77
  What I Knew 78
  Memories of Fort Morgan Road 80
  Bedfellows 81
  Traffic 83
  Ten Years Gone 84
  What's a River? 86
  Ballast 87
  Tidelines 89
  Internal Combustion: A Primer 90
Credits 93
Acknowledgments 95
Title Index 97
First Line Index 100

*I can see the drifting offshore lights,
black posts where the pelicans brood.*

*And the light that used to shine
at night in my father's study
now shines as late in mine.*

—Louis Simpson "Working Late"

OED

Sleepless, I read from our good book

Bless Her Heart

The new hospice nurse lacks
stillness. She fidgets, prattles on

about the *Lord's light, a better place.*
Soon, Dad's eyebrows begin

their familiar waggle, the one that pronounces
just how done he is with her.

After days without a word, he finally speaks
(though his voice gutters, a flagging flame).

LO—QUA—CIOUS, he enunciates
looking to my mother, to me, then

searing the gape-mouthed nurse
with those cinder-gray eyes.

Above echoes of exhausted laughter
the word still blazes—ours to keep.

Cleaving

So fierce, this love, in these small hours—
as if hearts might beat back time's advances.

On death's bed, love is not cleaving to
but a cleaving from—from pain, from delirium.
Still, he won't let go, won't *turn loose*,

the words he hisses when we grab hold
to force pills on him. The sitters say

some patients hang on like this
(*tenacity*, he would have called it).
They tell us to give him permission.

My brother, sister, and I take turns:
You've done enough. Nothing changes

until my mother does the bravest thing
—climbs into his bed, spoons him
and whispers: *It's time. You can let go.*

After a Prolonged Illness

I don't know what to say
when the reporter pleads,
just give me something.

I know only what I can't:
that my father, party boss,
warhorse lawyer, legendary

for his force of will, waited
until the house reverted
to its appliance hum, until

my mother made one last
pharmacy run, until my sister
took her sons just far enough

from death's quiet pall
that they could play and shout
and be boys. I can't say

my brother dashed home
to shower, that my wife bought
groceries to feed us all again

then sat for hours with my
brokenhearted grandmother
who chain-smoked her grief.

And I certainly can't tell her
the only person in the room
was the young hospice nurse

who shouted for me. Or how
I felt for a pulse, then dropped
my ear to his still-warm chest

to listen—who knows for what—
the burr of his outboard's idle
the peal of a long wave breaking.

Panic Attack with Grief and Clavier

Like a hot shell casing
I drop each thought
—time moves in jerks
my mind won't let
me dwell on any one thing.

I can't get enough air
in my lungs and
I sense something's
about to happen
that I'm not going to like.

Every time I try to place
this uneasy feeling
my synapses misfire
as if to keep me from
what has me jangled.

I wrench my shoes off
snatch my shirt over my head
heap my clothes on the floor
and imagine unfastening my skin
to reveal glistening viscera

then close my eyes and feel
them burn. I should sleep
but keep typing—half-believing
I might still find something
vital between these words.

The Funeral Director's Eyes

Jammed in his gray face,
their light burned out, fallen in.
Did it happen like a light bulb:

Pop! then nothing? How much
grief funds another upsell—
pads death's already ample margin?

Still, I want his dimmed eyes
so I won't see my mother
(who can't get out of bed)

or the gaping hole in the Gulf
(namesake of Marquez's Macondo)
so big that satellites track

black plumes of oil from space
—or the bees in the walls
of the house at the river

we can't yet sell—all 150,000
stowaways droning between
its dormers—the whole house

become a great, thrumming skull.
When we climbed up to the attic
honey oozed through humming walls.

OED

Even though it's impossible
I know he conjured that squall.

Perhaps the fuss embarrassed him
—or maybe it was his idea of a joke.

July's sky scorched to blue haze.
A soaring gray thunderhead

scoured the air above the funeral.
Cold, marble-fat raindrops pelted

down as a black ring of umbrellas
sprouted and scattered from his grave.

That night I dreamt my father walked
his camellia garden with a basketful

of pink and white blooms crooked
in the elbow of his pale-blue corduroy.

I woke under the dream's sway and nearly
dashed into summer's teeming dark.

Months later, I am pinned beneath
his naked corpse and wake gasping.

Sleepless, I read from our good book
that *grief* stems from the same root

as *gravity* and understand how much
further I must bear the heft of loss.

Lessons in the Hidden Tongue

The dream is always the same:
I'm washing my hands at work
when I realize the room is humming.

I see them in the mirror: bees—
a few, a dozen, now a cloud.

One lights on my white Oxford.
Though I should be afraid
I bend to splash my eyes.

When I stand, the face looking back
is no longer mine. Always

its eyes burned out, fallen in.
Cold air rushes into their sockets
then the bees plunge in:

a score, a hundred, a thousand.
Each time, I startle awake, clawing

at my face. But soon I hope to find
my way to the dream's end,
to wake—with my limbs jangling—

my head thrumming with life,
and the taste of honey on my tongue.

His Sky-Blue Tie

Weeks before my brother's wedding, I mined
the dictionary's rich veins, searching for spells
to conjure our father's lambent drawl.

He loved the ways ritual blurred
time's bright edges—how language
could weave past into future.

In his wake, I became the family's word-miller,
penning godless prayers at holidays.
So, at the rehearsal dinner, I let guests

warm the room, cocksure of my incantation.
But when I stood, the words I'd burnished
crumbled in my throat like flakes of ash.

Though I'd knotted our father's wedding tie
(sky-blue with paisleys like fresh-caught fish)
in my best Windsor, buffed his wingtips

beetle-black, even pocketed the last
of his mother's Irish linen handkerchiefs,
my invocation failed. I'd misjudged my talent

to unravel time, to bring him—if briefly—back.
As my mother rose to toast the newlyweds,
I rang with failure like my outstretched glass.

How My Father Became a Boat

My three-year-old nephew watches
boats zip up and down the river.
Pale hulls rush over tannin-browned water
and the air buzzes with engine noise.

He is thrilled by all of them:
Where he's going?
he asks, again and again.
Beside us, my father's skiff
swings in its sling above the water.

The boy points: *Pop's boat?*
Yes, I say.
Where Pop is?
I wrestle his question
but he answers first:
Pop's dead.

Then, pointing at the boat,
he asks: *What Pop's doing?*
before pronouncing:
Him resting.
Remembering Vardaman
I think: *My mother is a fish*

and smile—knowing my father
would have liked to become a boat.
We sit quietly for a few moments
before the boy stuns me with a question
I have never once considered: *What's a river?*

Calculations from the Moral Arc

More troubled steps in America's sick arithmetic

Where Does a River End?

A tidewater koan to soothe my mind
on the long drive home, some place to go

besides grief. I let muscle memory
steer the backroads while traveling the river

in my mind: east past Point Legere
—curling back west at Slaughter's Bend

before dipping south into the basin
then meandering southeast by Hall's Mill Creek

and the marina. Just before Mobile Bay
a concrete arc hums with traffic

traveling in both directions,
like the brackish river it crosses,

like the word for this place: *estuary*
from the Latin *æstus*, where the tide

bubbles and boils, where there
are no still points, only turning worlds.

Hurricane Lilies

All day my brother and I hear his voice
as we tend to this season's rituals:
buying bagged ice and bottled water
winching his boat above the storm surge
snugging its corners with knots he taught us.

By sunset, the breeze has walked from west to east.
Backwinded, the night sounds strange—
its leaves murmur in unfamiliar tongues.

Only a handful of out-of-cycle cicadas scrape
the night's edges. In the Gulf, a susurration builds
a tiding. An untiring Leviathan churns north—
its dreamless eye staring twenty miles wide.

At supper, Mom gives guilty thanks
the storm has shifted, and none of us can avoid
looking toward his chair. Afterward, we brothers
sip bourbon on the wharf and trade memories.

When we run out of words and whiskey
we head to bed. Red spider lilies sway
in the blustering dark, marking the void
that held our great grandparents' home.

—*Hurricane Lilies*, Dad called them:
August blooms proclaiming *Hurricane Summer*
—the Gulf South's secret season—when tongues
of lightning burn through thunderheads
like slow fuses, when the air turns thick as flesh.

Calculations from the Moral Arc

This is the Black Belt: old cotton country—
a once-fertile crescent that cleaves the state in two.
As we bend along Highway 69 through a town
time can't decide to forget or remember
my mind is three hours south, trying to work out
how many round trips to the river remain

when a blur slices past us across double-yellow.
Cops are scarce here. Everyone knows
about the law—same way they know about equality
and unicorns. Which is to say, no one expects much.
Though the courthouse hosts a monument
to the Confederate dead, there are no battle flags,

at least in town. Bloody Lowndes stands down US 80
where Carmichael stoked Black Power's first fires.
Plantation ruins ossify next to shotgun shacks
that slouch toward housing projects, where people
were made slaves, prison labor, and sharecroppers
before they became sawmill workers, catfish farmers.

Vesey became Turner, then Jimmie Lee Jackson.
Even now—with both the vote and guns—
Black folk do all they can just to hold their own.
There are no jobs here, nothing to live off.
Generations on, the ledger is deep in the red.
I grieve anew that I cannot ask my father: *What now?*

This is the worst stretch I can recall.
All this subtraction, this division, it adds up—
more troubled steps in America's sick arithmetic.
For the first time, I despair that these accounts
might never reconcile, no matter how we strive
to solve for that more perfect union.

The Lesson

Storm clouds piled high
but we thought little of the thunder
till the rain turned white

whipped to froth by the tornado
we couldn't see but felt
like bones grinding in the soil beneath us.

Maybe it was atavism (or beer)
but my friend and I didn't shelter
in the tub like the weatherman said.

Instead, we leaned into stinging rain
straining to glimpse
what might teach us to die.

Backroads Ovid

I'm following a line of storms home.
Even before dawn, the highway's
still so hot from yesterday
a quilt of steam hovers over it.

Thunderbolts reveal the entire
landscape in instants of daylight.
Trees and grass blaze green
then vanish. A mile out
lightning pulses deep in pillowy clouds
like the neurons firing this memory.

Worn asphalt looms gray in my headlights
as the odometer spins, relentlessly milling
backroad atopia into something taut
with possibility. Suddenly, I feel as though

the road's low drone is unwinding
some celestial mainspring—that soon
night's clockwork will unlock day's.
And somehow (even in my untidy mind)
the jagged gears of these last years
begin to mesh with those yet to come.

In motion at least, I can imagine something
like my way. So I urge my car west,
keep the sun from my rearview, and pray:
Run slowly, horses of the night.
Grant me a few more miles of gray road.

Sleeping Porch

Air sighs through bellied screens
—thick—like the heat that bears
down on me. I peel the sheet off

and listen to my bare soles whisper
through the grass and down
to the wharf. In moon-silver dark

I lower the boat and pray
neighbors won't hear the engine.
I plane and make wide, arcing

turns toward the Bay. A mile
into the channel's winking lights
I cut the motor. Tones from markers

and waves slapping the gunwales
the only sounds now. I dive
into cool water and open my eyes

astonished to see my moonlit hands
and kick down toward the soft silt
just beyond light's reach, then surge

up in great strokes to the watery moon.
I lunge past the surface, my lungs
raw with effort, aching with life.

Evinrude Ode

Another Black Belt backroad
between the river and the college:
For nearly twenty miles
I've been stuck behind a log truck.

Its orange flag taunts my headlights
sprays splinters of pine bark
bouncing across the silver hood
clattering across the windshield.

There's a straightaway ahead
where I'll pass him and reset
my night's soundtrack to the hum
of four tires on worn blacktop

which summons the many hours
I hummed along with his outboards
running from Navy Cove to Sand Island
from Cedar Point to Petit Bois.

Bumping along Highway 69
in the dark, I can almost hear
the wake's hiss, nearly see him
at the binnacle in his khaki shorts,

Marlboros and trusty Montblanc
stuffed in the breast pocket
of his faded red T-shirt, his silver hair
flickering in the wind like pale fire.

Recipe with Healthy Crime

for my mother

Ingredients:

    1 slice of bacon—thicker is better
    1 copy of Dave Brubeck's *Take Five*
        (if unavailable, Miles Davis's *Kind of Blue*)
    2 cups each of: onion, celery, and bell pepper
    1 copy of *The Collected Works of Eudora Welty*
    A bottle of dry white wine, very cold
    As much seafood as you can afford
    1 flower of blue flame

One: Cook the bacon in a large saucepan until the fat renders. Remove it, reserving the drippings, then take a bite. Feed the rest to your dogs.

    She's teaching me to find my way
    around downtown's sainted streets.
    Today's the day the city secrets away
    its festive purple and gold signs:
    No parking 2 hours before or after parade
    to reinstall their pale, Waspy cousins.
    We stop to swap seats and she points
    to a carnival sign on the ground—I'm afraid,
    but she doesn't even pause to look.
    She just drops it on the back seat.

Two: Sauté the onions, celery, and bell pepper in the bacon drippings. Consider the more radical implications of "Creole Trinity."

> My mother teaches me that a bribe
> is as much about timing as value.
> The garbagemen keep ignoring
> the ancient window air conditioner
> we are trying to get rid of—
> until my mother plots to ply them.
> She waits for a hot, muggy day,
> then as the truck pulls up, she stands
> by the rusting carcass and hoists
> a six-pack of tall-boys—chilled, of course.

Three: As the onion, celery, and bell pepper sauté, add a heavy pinch of "Blue Rondo à la Turk." Take care the 9/8 time doesn't pulverize the peppers.

> Studying abroad one heartbroken winter,
> the lesson nearly escapes me. After dinner
> in Paris with my folks, I finally want to see
> a friend, have a nightcap—maybe even two.
> She kisses my cheek, palms me some cash.
> I don't grasp it—try to hand it back: *In case someone wants your wallet*, she whispers.
> Years later I know she wanted to teach me
> what she knew from her own blue devils:
> Manage what fear you cannot quell.

Four: Retrieve wine from freezer. Sip while consulting Miss Welty to taste.

> My mother keeps watch in the breezy night
> as I snip a flag from a defunct ferry:
> a gift for a friend. Like the sign, it's her find,
> but I am beginning to feel more thrill than fear
> in these moments, absorbing her sense
> for which rules to break. I learn ways
> to make her recipe my own—practice
> listening to my instincts—and find myself
> adding more daring to every dish,
> and reserving a pinch of mischief for garnish.

Of Time and Tide

We trickle in at Christmas
and take turns saying goodbye
to the river. My mother is moving
back to town after New Year's.

From the wharf, I can see
to the silty bottom until the sun dips
too low for its light to reach.
I sit, read the news, and watch

as the sky catches Maxfield Parrish fire.
A local reporter thinks he's found
the Clotilda, the last ship
to steal Africans into America.

The owner did it on a cruel bet
—burned his ship in the Tensaw Delta
to hide his crime. Photos show
rows of dark timbers thrusting

through the water's surface,
mud-slick at winter's lowest tide.
And for an instant, I see
a fire-blacked ribcage

streaked with silt—an invisible heart
beating within it, marking
generations lost in the ebb
of untold tides—and counting down.

A Ripple of Hope

A ripple sings forth when we stand up

A Ripple of Hope

with lines after RFK's Day of Affirmation Address

They'll have to screw his coffin shut
my father growled the day George Wallace died.
The ghoul who fueled his power by stoking hate
white hot, who sneered at equality

from the schoolhouse door, who hoisted
the Battle Flag over the capitol to troll
Bobby Kennedy, where it blazed for thirty years.

I was a kid when it finally came down—
I didn't understand how the lie of the Lost Cause
soothed the comfortable classes. So, I asked

my father—among Camelot's last knights
in Alabama—wasn't this just history?
He hissed: *Does the swastika still fly in Berlin?*
then he sat me down to teach me how

the mountaintop became the valley of the shadow
of Bull Connor's Bombingham, how hate turned
dogs and firehoses on the Children's Crusade—

that the past is a prison the South is afraid to leave
(even though white folks hold the keys).
After Dad died, I found RFK's words in his study

and thrilled to read what he'd taught me:
a ripple sings forth when we stand up.
And when enough of us dare, chords of hope
surge high enough to sweep down what divides us.

Greatest of These

Back at the same square, my wife and I
sweat through our third vigil this summer.

This time, because the slow poison
of watching men murdered for being Black
has killed yet another Black man.

A steady sprinkle nearly breaks the heat,
and my lapsed Presbyterian skin itches
when a pastor asks us to pray with strangers.

We bow our heads, watch concrete sip drizzle,
and then, miraculously, we start to believe

we might escape unshriven. Until they appear:
Bruce wears ostrich-skin boots, pale Wranglers.

Nancy sports drawn-on brows, a look of wonder.
They're good people. Though we admit we're not
church-folk, they pray with and for (and a little *at*) us.

Then, because he must, Bruce witnesses.
He covers us with his great black umbrella, which
he likens to God. It's a kindness; we thank them.

When we don't give in, he groans: *Why are you here?*
I tell him: *We have doubts about God—but not Love.*

Eye of the Storm

Thick, tropical winds
strip leaves from branches
in a pelting, rainless storm

that shouts like thousands
of pages of history turning.
Even this far inland, trees

still speak hurricane.
Its strange combination
of whispers and shouts

rattles summer-green leaves.
But this is only the overture,
a season newly begun.

The strongest storms
always cross from Africa,
off The Gambia and Senegal,

past Île de Gorée, where
La Porte Sans Retour
at the Maison des Esclaves

at last stands open.
Here, deadly gales spawned
long before the conquistadors

stole the word, *hurac'an*
from the Taino: *the wind's center*
—the hurricane's raging eye.

Tonight, as one storm
disintegrates over the South,
descendants of stolen people

gather across America, towering
like thunderheads to form another.
Wave upon wave of Black suffering,

Black frustration, Black anger
lash the country with storm-bands
that have built since Jamestown.

And tonight, after 400 years
of being shouted down by whiteness,
protestors recount centuries of struggle

in an all-too corporeal tongue:
each verb quick as a raised fist,
every noun obvious as an upturned palm.

After all this time, after everything
taken, who wouldn't cry out
in the language of the unheard?

Consulting the Book of Rumination

Over a year into our slow-motion apocalypse,
nothing ever ends. The seas never quite boil—

the asteroid flies just wide—the final cataclysm
keeps missing its cue. Instead, a virus seethes

around the world, fueling fear that burns sleep
to cinders. In the wakeful dark, our debts and doubts

gather in woolly clouds, blue as the bruises we nurse
—those hidden hurts that help keep us human.

When yet another Black man dies, crying out
that he can't breathe, Americans show up

in numbers—despite COVID's chokehold—
to begin bearing witness to the Lost Cause's lies.

Next, hurricanes jump the alphabet, and as we cope
with the ever-growing cone of our uncertainty, we ask:

How many more before Omega? In August,
fires scorch California skies nightmare shades

of orange and ash rains across the country.
Before democracy stumbles by gaslight,

a diminutive collar pens her final dissent.
There's simply too much doom to scroll.

In the endless wheel of another dreamless night,
we strive to keep the mind from bending against itself,

from corrupting the thrill of longing into the dread of
   loss.
We pore over the Book of Rumination to confirm

this next threat is just the latest near miss
and continue practice imagining impossible things:

pillars of fire, tongues of flame, a future where
the catch in our throats is born not of fear but wonder.

Plague Summer, College Town

Another night, golf-cart rickshaws
would chuck students between bars.

But tonight, I parse the busy layers
of this season's strange silence:

its never-ending insect chirr—
the streetlights' menacing buzz,

the blessed drone of air conditioners,
each a valence around a hushed core.

Some summer to come, I may miss this—
how the sensory load crosses from heard

to felt. But this year it aches of loss,
of lives and parts of lives razed from memory.

Tonight, though, I bob in a thunderstorm's
cool wake. Magnolias tinge summer's swelter

with notes of sweet cream and citrus.
As the storm rumbles away, the rain's last

drops tick down waxy green leaves
onto brown husks from seasons past.

The rich scent of a nameless spice rises
redolent of decay—yet fat with life.

Be it Ever So Humble

I never meant to stay here.
It's too far from brackish water,
though not far enough to outrun my ghosts.

I doubt I would have survived Mobile
—watching Folly chase Death
around Life's ruined column,
enduring countless variations on:
I remember your father.

Even my brother moved over the Bay,
hoping those haints couldn't follow
him across running water.

I miss my hometown but hate it, too.
For every live-oak-lined street,
for every pelican's wheeling dive,
there's a hum of dread I just can't quiet,
a wound that aches from nearness.

So, I live here, in this almost-college town,
where the sky fades tornado-green
too easily and too often, secretly pining

for the weeks and months between semesters,
when Tuscaloosa echoes like an empty movie set,
when the hive of my droning mind can calm,
and we townies nod to each other at the grocery
    store—
thankful to have the place to ourselves for a while.

Where's Your Accent?

A question strangers ask
that calls back classrooms
and conference tables

where a vowel I smudged
or an *R* I left on the page
drew glances—and the flush

that blazed up my neck
as peers lowered my IQ
to match my drawl.

I keep it in a bus-locker
I usually breeze. But under
my breath I can't help but pray
Saint Eudora Welty,
Saint Zora Neale Hurston,
anoint my tongue

with the perfect malediction
to stop this latest fool
    like a hard *G*.

Heat Lightning

I just called the cops on a party
for the first time ever. I kind of feel bad,
but it's too late, too stifling, for all that.
Heat lightning teases from the offing,
and the air is pregnant with humidity.

Underage drinking is one thing,
but I draw the line at karaoke.
Geezer, they'll call me. Maybe I am.
I am old enough to remember when
people read the reports on the weather radio.

My favorite was the good-ole boy whose
deific baritone foretold *thunder-boomers*
rumbling up the Bay. I'd stay up late
watching lightning paint the clouds purple
before it poked the water with crooked fingers.

Maybe someday, I'll be too old
to hear caterwauling neighbors,
but I'll never forget the sound of thunder
rolling across breaking waves—like god
tumbling down a staircase, drunk and singing.

Ebb Tide

It seemed she might never stop rising

Elegy for Hustle-man

for James William Griffin

There was no handshake. No, *I'm James—
folks call me Hustle-man.* Bucket in hand,
you skipped that and car-washed your way

to pocket money. Hard as you worked,
people offered you jobs, places to stay
to pull it together. But they never quite got

that you preferred sleeping rough, how you
thrived on the hustle: scrounging and selling,
hauling your way to neighborhood fixture.

Even though it's been years since
the cops found you gunshot, I still hear you
scold me every time I make a sandwich:

Aw, come on, man, don't scrimp on the mayo.
I miss that voice, all the nights you crooned
the Pointer Sisters' "Fire" block by block.

But the main thing, James, what I'll never forget
is what you taught me about dignity.
Even when I blew you off, had nothing to haul,

or didn't buy your latest dumpster find, you'd
refuse my apologies, silence me with a quick
side-eye, and say: *God never made anything sorry.*

Ship-breaking

for RJL

You died an old man's death, even though you weren't.
I remember you just before: your loud plaid robe
and chromed cane (understatement never was your
    style).

The engines start with a rough thrum.
Groaning winches weigh anchors.
The ship's prow plows through
dark waves, splintering moonlight.

I looked at your hollowed cheeks, yellowing skin
so I wouldn't see your legs, swollen
from the death your liver spread.

Under the full moon, spring tides
shrink the shore to a glowing crescent.
The ship steams toward the beach
until the bow-wave surges inland.

As I touch the casket lid, sandy soil the priest cast
catches the whorls of my fingertips. And I hear Latin
before recognizing the voice is mine.

The behemoth does not stop.
Hundreds of tons shift their burden from
sea to sand with a sound that has no name:
the ship falls impossibly still.

Not the Pater Noster, but the schoolboy curse
you taught me. And as my flask chuckles
I try to believe that somewhere you're laughing.

At dawn, ship-breakers pick the carcass clean.
The Leviathan glows deep into the night as torches
burn slabs of the hull free, bit by blazing bit.

Hope's Hollow Bones

for BB & Two-Step

That guy from school
the one everyone knew
was beautiful. The one

who glowed electric
when he outshone others
with his long-limbed grace

—the one who exuded
instinctive cool: Bit by bit
his body now betrays him.

After some bump jostles
his too-taut spine, or when
morning's low sun hooks his eye,

weeks' long migraines flare
—driving him into a dark room
where desolation would billow

unchecked. But somehow
he holds fast. Though loss
throbs inside the normal
he now must live

every morning he can,
he climbs a ladder as far
from pain as its rungs reach

to practice hope,
the kind birds summon
each time they take flight.

Memorial Day

for Phil Beidler

In the supermarket foyer I take a buggy
under tricolor bunting to honor
the long weekend's sales, and remember

a friend's gibe: *dulce et decorum est*
translates to: *20% off, one day only.*
Welcome to the land of the free, home
of the beer rebranded *Freedom* for summer.

Of course, today I bump into my old mentor
once a young lieutenant in Vietnam.
I ask after his wife, their young daughter—

and he teases that my wife, the biologist,
must grasp reproduction even if I don't.
We laugh and shake hands before
he shuffles into summer's early heat.

I know I should follow him out,
thank him, pay my respects to those he lost
(during and after), instead I push
my cart into the store and turn

down row after ordered row
before I realize that *lieutenant*
means *placeholder* and curse
leaders who send others' kids to die.

Elegy with Black Holes and Hawking Radiation

for my grandmother

Strictly speaking, there's no such thing
—at least no *black* and no *holes*—
but how else do we fathom lapsed stars
that raze matter, light, even time?

Since we can't see nothing, we seek heat,
search for mirages that speak presence
but mean absence. That's how we find
the isn't that is. But black holes,

though ruthless, aren't wholly efficient.
Some of what falls in evaporates as ardor.
Physics demands all that ever was
contains a record of its birth, its death.

Centuries, millennia, eons boil off
in roiling clouds of ones and zeroes,
but somewhere in every destruction
seethes a testament to all that came before.

Tidewater Hedge-Witch

for my grandmother

I. Sympathetic Magic

I woke to a scream and ran
to her in tears. Mimi cocked an ear
and purred, *Oh honey,*

that's just an old screech owl.
Tucking me in, she knotted the corner
of my sheet. That owl stopped cold.

A stronger spell bound Mimi's house
against harm. She chain-smoked
menthol 100s (Salems, of course)

making towers of glowing ash
that teetered into carpets and couches,
sacks stuffed with worked crosswords.

She drew her power from reaching
elbow deep in the earth—planting
and transplanting, nursing green things

to flourishing. Damn growing zones.
She summoned whatever she sought
to grow from seed, slip, or scion.

Some magic overflowed the tin pails
she kept to catch her famed elixir:
rainwater from thunderstorms.

After squalls, we'd dash between
her chuckling downspouts,
dosing her frail dogwoods,

treat the latest sapling grown
from seeds spirited past Customs
with a grin and grandmotherly guile.

My memory conflates the pails'
fish-belly hue with the water's power
—fading like a fresh-caught fish.

II. Cruel Magic

Mimi taught my sister to read palms
the summer she turned ten.
One Sunday, driving home

from church in a vast Oldsmobile,
Emily sat up front, seatbelt cinched
across her skinny hips, dark hair

shimmering to her shoulders. She read
her namesake's palm at a stop-light:
It says here we should have an aunt.

In the breathless car, Mimi told us
how she'd lost a daughter.
This was her cruelest magic: surviving

—even when she no longer meant to.
She outlived her mean-drunk ex-husband,
her coven of bridge-playing widows,

and her only child. Weeks before
her funeral, my sister heard her
curse herself for not dying sooner.

But Mimi's not quite gone. Whenever
she wants to weigh-in, we catch a whiff
of menthol, then the desk she left us

pops and groans. I'm waiting for it
to share its secrets like her giant car.
I stomped its squishy brakes

on the way to have it serviced
before we gave it to her sitter,
and summoned a supernatural gift

from under the seat: a pint bottle
of bourbon whose gold-fringed label
and amber liquid glowed in the sun.

What the Dead Want

A persistent sun roiled the air
above rain-darkened headstones
the first time I considered
what they want from us.

Spring storms had flooded
Magnolia Cemetery's every fold
and hollow. When school let out
we scaled the cyclone fence

and leapt into rainwater-filled ditches
to catch enormous crawfish
flushed from overtopped storm drains
to run and tussle between graves.

No one saw him—the deputy
who materialized among us—
like the ghosts we never thought to fear.
My friends froze, glowing with shame.

But I fled, pumping skinny fists
as the lawman bawled us out
for being all-too alive.
I topped the chattering chain links

and squelched four blocks home.
I was old enough to know this:
What I'd done was wrong
and just what the dead would want.

Ebb Tide

Above the dying mall's parking lot
flocks of gulls in from the Bay soar
on thermals that roil the air. Their cries
ring so loud I turn up the radio

as I drive home from the rehab
where my mother dozes, fitfully.
A port-wine bruise blots her forearm,
and another (that she won't let me see)

throbs across four broken ribs—
forcing a gasp whenever she moves.
Neither of us can fathom the walker
she pushes, or where the woman went

who landed boats in three-foot swells
by timing her jump from the bow
up to the wharf so that it seemed
she might never stop rising.

Keeping the Sacraments

The only faith I was born to

My Drug of Choice Is the Dictionary

In loss, others may turn
to stronger stuff, but I confess,
I crave its whiffs of history,

its glimpses of meaning
—the illusion of order
its columns uphold.

But the high it delivers is not
always as white as its margins,
as dark as its letters. *Aftermath*

hints at a grand solution
but only means *second harvest*,
a last pass at a field's yield.

And then you cross it: *Threshold*.
Despite its promise
of etymological magic,

it, too, disappoints: *Doorsill*,
sources universally render it
(even its vowels depressing).

Thresh: the blow that divides
wheat from chaff—
Hold: from a word so old

we've lost its first sense:
maybe where to stomp
to keep muck outdoors—

a final line to separate work
from home: the place
we nourish our treasure.

How to Speak with Ghosts

Do not trouble us idly.
Our sleep is restless enough
without demands to waltz
in and out of your dreams on cue.

Instead, bind your worries
until they become so snarled
there's no telling end from beginning
—until the cool heft of logic fails.

Then call on us. Never mind dreams:
Listen for the whisper in your bones.
Ours is the hidden tongue that sounds
inside the murmur of blood and breath

And when dawn comes—blade-bright—
you will know there is no unraveling
your misgivings, no untying these cares.
You will know a thing outside of reason:

      To slice the knot.

Keeping the Sacraments

Each day I offer this kinetic prayer
to make myself his echo: a nib, a lock-blade,
my loud bandanna for his
linen handkerchief, penknife, and Montblanc.

I stretch his wingtips on shoetrees,
fray his old twill collars against
my bull-neck, and knot his sky-blue tie
for my brother's second wedding.

Even if I fear him still
in my raised voice—feel the shame
of wielding words like a fist—
I thank him for teaching me

to mine the dark-lettered strata
of our dictionary's Bible-thin pages.
I keep the sacraments of language,
the only faith I was born to.

Just as memory's edge
heals because it cuts away,
forgiveness kindles flames
to burn our hurt to curling ash.

Grief demands these awful symmetries:
that we twin sentiments beyond
balance, that we learn how
deeply loss plumbs love's depths.

Memory's Edges

His flesh made word

      he could do nothing

for fear someone

      might translate him.

Stories best forgotten

      etched his fascia,

burned in his bones.

      Their tales muted

who he must become

      —dulled the chant

echoing in his blood:

      hold fast—let go,

      hold fast—let go.

He nearly gave in

      before solving its riddle:

Memory is a blade

      that cleaves away

as much as it preserves,

      the means to rewrite

the chapters of his flesh,

    to remember himself

by cutting new stories

    —letter by letter—

in slivers of living bone.

The Sacrament of Solitude

Whorls of rain drum the year away
under violet skies. It's Sunday,
and I haven't spoken in days.

But this is not grief, it is time
consecrated to becoming, a sabbath
hewn from the cult of endless work.

I sit by the fireplace
in my father's old club chair
trading long sips between

a tumbler of bourbon and meltwater
and pages full of words.
Outside, streetlights bloom: orbs of sparkling rain.

Within, I devote myself to gathering
wool enough to build thunderheads
that will light the night for miles.

The Benediction

Unlike my wont to worry every edge
like a tongue seeks a chipped tooth
my father sought out uncertainty
—happy of any *if* that became a *when*.

He expected I'd feel the same charge
in not quite knowing. Instead, I watched
the water's dark mirror ripple the moon.

He understood how much I feared failing
him—how uneasy I was to bear his name.
But more mischief than I imagined
squalled in his storm-gray eyes.

I never understood the thrill he found
charging into darkness—until he materialized
from the trilling night while a friend and I drank
wharf-warm beers. His baritone cleaved the air

with a blasphemous benediction: *I trust you
will misbehave*, just before he vanished
into a blue puff of cigarette smoke
and the faerie music of ice tinkling in his scotch.

Vessels

My brother and I rig fenders
on what was our father's boat.

Our mother steps from shade
to sun to remind, to instruct.

A widow once more, she wears
a broad-brimmed hat, dark glasses:

the boat another body of her beloved.
She's sold it to a young father upriver

whose sons will learn the way to care
for a boat like my brother and I did.

I watch our hands tie half-hitches
and fuse frayed ends as we were taught.

Turned pink by the noon's high sun,
we drop fenders over his gunwales

a final time—just the right height
to protect his sides. Pallbearers anew

we dress him in his funeral best—
shipshape, ready for the next voyage.

Reading the Gulf

foam-topped waves roll ashore
like pages of an endless book

What I Knew

We were brothers—wrestling
the long, taut line between

rivalry and devotion: Who could
jump farther, climb higher, fall harder?

Who would invent the next game
just dangerous enough to be fun?

We were boys—struggling to grow
into our outsized confidence.

Older, my job was to know better.
Instead, I made a bow from a lattice slat

notched wooden dowels for arrows
snipped fins from silver-gray duct tape.

We took turns shooting over each other
until the blunt tip raised a purple welt.

I apologized over and over, and as soon
as you stopped crying, you swore

not to tell. But Mom knew already—
before the dark spot bloomed

into a vast, grackle-black shiner
that took weeks to fully fade.

At nine, an allergic reaction burnt
every bit of you to scab or blister.

You spiked a fever so high the hospital
packed your head in ice to keep

your brain from baking. I remember
your red eyes ringed with fear,

their sheen of tears. Dad summoned
a procession of doctors who bled you,

poked and scoped you, all in the name
of doing no harm, because fixing things

(even if by main-strength and awkwardness)
was how our father showed he cared.

When we were teenagers, he took us fishing
as the Gulf shook off the last of a storm.

Hours we pitched between whitecaps
—though we knew nothing would bite.

When a rogue wave tossed the boat,
a three-inch hook swung free and bit deep

into the meat of your pale forearm.
This time you didn't cry, not even

when Dad fetched the rusty bait-pliers.
You just looked at me with wide, sad eyes

that said how sick you were of love that hurt
and I knew to turn the boat around.

Memories of Fort Morgan Road

pelicans plunge into tideline foam

gas tank fumes foretell outboard whine

anchor-chain drips blue-gray silt

spinning spoon catches Spanish mackerel

teal waves break over jade sandbars

fine sand pricks legs tanned brown

cooler-lid creak renders ice-cold beer

cotton-candy clouds part for blazing sunset

gas-lantern mantle guides flounder gig

sweet corn steams while whitefish broils

bottle rocket pops punctuate sparkler fizz

lukewarm shower flows into sunburned sleep

Bedfellows

Yesterday it was 65 and sunny
and tomorrow it will be again,

but today the sun is away visiting
other clients. A north wind pushes

the river out into the Bay, revealing
gunmetal mud flats that set off

gold blades of marsh grass against
oyster-shell skies. The kind of cold

that makes hands ache, freezes
fingers stiff. I hear shotguns roar

from duck blinds and remember
the hunting camp in the woods

west of Bay Minette, where
my father's law partner tried

to humble him with an invitation
to the family's sharecropper cabin,

its paint chipped the color of forgetting.
I don't think I ever felt so cold

as I did that night, the two of us
shivering on ancient mattresses

covered with navy-striped ticking
that stunk of dust and stale sweat.

I might have been thirteen—
embarrassed of being cold, worse,

of having a body. I never felt
so loved as when he asked me

to sleep back-to-back, doubling
our warmth against January's chill.

Traffic

All our childhood's monsoon weekends,
when my brother, sister, and I ran out
of games to play, toys to play with

—once we grew tired of gazing into
the TV's hypnotic eye, we'd pry open
the pocket doors to our father's study

—inchmeal—convinced he couldn't see
our skinny fingers, hear our whispers.
Inside, we'd snake across the busy rug

and hide behind his red club chair,
or else beneath his vast desk, its slab
of green glass floating on a cork gasket.

After eons listening to his blue pen
(and then his red one) scritch across
yellow legal pads, we'd grow restive,

grousing from our all-too-visible cover
that we were bored, there was nothing to do.
On good days, he'd shush us and slide

the hi-fi's mahogany top open to drop
The Beatles, or else Handel, on the turntable
—messiahs we adored. But secretly,

we hoped for the days he'd roust us out
and mock-scold our lack of imagination
and purr our favorite curse: *Go play in traffic.*

Ten Years Gone

I. Spring

It must be March again—the crows argue
how best to invoke the rites of spring.
Knuckled crape myrtles stub at clearing skies

and Japanese magnolia petals litter the streets
like paper from firecrackers. Spring is upon us
—its fuse spitting green sparks.

II. Summer

July in Alabama is heat seasoned with sound.
Even before dawn, you can feel it
coiling beneath the pavement, set to strike.

It's the constant drone of A/C compressors
the cicadas' insistent chorus sawing the air
the chatter of sprinklers—just out of reach.

III. Fall

The car tumbles through the year's last leaves
an autumnal comet. We lose an hour tonight:
Daylight stealing time, my brother calls it.

But for now, I scud before the dying light
and hope that someplace beyond the offing
all those lost hours wait for us.

IV. Winter

Winter doesn't come here—not really—
instead, it rains. We don coats out of respect
light the odd fire against the chill, the short days.

This is the season of unfinished business
when memories gather in drifts between us—
metes and bounds that mark living from dying.

What's a River?

Another tidewater koan:
a question so trenchant
only a child could ask it.

An idea so rich we mine it
to approach complexity's throne:
currents that drive oceans,

winds that girdle the globe,
hydrogen plumes that birth galaxies
—energy flowing through time.

Meaning a family makes a river:
the people we add, those we lose
(the ones we must let go)
become its flow, its ebb.

Ours the privilege to buoy memories
of those who came before
into futures we cannot know.

Ballast

In those raw first days
grief's weight lifted
only in sleep and broke
on me like a black wave
each time I woke.

It began as anguish
but after months, seasons,
years, grief transformed
me. During my journey
under the yoke of loss,

I sensed its load ease.
After a time, I found
something akin to comfort
in its dumb heft.

When ill tides turned,
I relied on my grief as ballast,
a keel to true my course.

Because the pain of loss
gauges love's full depth,
I should have known

grief carried messages
in its voids and hollows,
that those we lose
travel with us in our loss—

how, with patient study,
we might learn to hear them
—even feel a kind of lightness—
despite grief's awful weight.

Tidelines

Beneath the sounds
of blood and breath

a formless organ
a heart pumping time

tugs to tell us
(even miles from the sea)

when the tide
is ebbing or flowing.

Internal Combustion: A Primer

Packing list:

> 1 thermos of coffee—brewed black as forgetting
> 1 copy (dog-eared) of Partridge's *Origins*—for
>   saltwater etymologies
> 6 gallons of gas—mixed 50:1, wonder and terror
> assorted fishing lures and treble hooks, ground
>   sharp as memory

One: Grip primer bulb, feel where salt and sun have pitted its black rubber. Pump until firm. Turn ignition key.

Still Life with Weather Radio

> When I find the photo in his desk
> from the old beach house
> I fall deep into memory's orbit.
>
> It's the kind of picture only he took
> —no one in frame, no context—
> just objects on the green Formica bar.
>
> Beside the sunflower-yellow cooler
> the weather radio's red eye peers
> at the curled top-sheet of a legal pad
>
> where a note in his jagged script
> explains how to calculate tides
> from Mobile Point to Point Legere.

Two: Jiggle throttle to be sure boat is in neutral. Choke as you turn ignition again. Swear under your breath.

Boats of Ash

    My father, freshly shaved, smells
    of Barbasol and Marlboros. I am six.
    He looms over me as he teaches

    me to tie my school tie. I feel
    his cigarette blaze by my ear,
    hear its tobacco crackle.

    Flecks of ash float down on my tie
    —tiny pale boats on a sea
    of navy (with red and white stripes).

    In our reflections, I watch his gray eyes
    scan behind gold-rimmed aviators.
    He sips coffee, assesses his handiwork.

Three: Curse yourself for not knowing more about outboards. Turn key a third time. Listen to the flywheel's hyena laugh.

How to Know Impossible Things

    Lately, when I dream of my father
    we happen upon one other
    on some street I don't know

    or in a house I've never been inside.
    We're surprised to meet like this
    but recognize each other instantly.

Always, I feel a twinge of embarrassment
because he doesn't realize he's dead
(just the kind of loophole he'd find)

I know then, the way in dreams,
we know impossible things, that my duty
is to keep him from finding out.

Four: Invoke gods you don't even believe in. Turn key again. Cheer when engine sputters to life and coughs itself smooth.

Reading The Gulf

Nothing moves like open water:
whitecaps break, the wind
crosshatches its surface

like miles of hurried script
dashed onto paper
in defiance of forgetting.

This image arrives at sleep's coast:
foam-topped waves roll ashore
like pages of an endless book.

I dream chapter after chapter
of moonlit spindrift and feast on words
so grand only the sea can sound them out.

Credits

Grateful acknowledgement is made to the editors of the following publications where earlier versions of these poems first appeared (several under different titles and with different formatting):

"Elegy for Hustle-Man"—*Anti-Heroin Chic* Grief & Loss (November 2020)

"OED"—*Cider Press Review*, Vol. 24, No. 2 (October 2022)

"The Funeral Director's Eyes"—*Cider Press Review*, Vol. 24, No. 3 (December 2022)

"After a Prolonged Illness"—*Comstock Review*, Vol. 36, No. 2 (January 2023)

"Ten Years Gone"—*Kindred*, Vol. 1, No. 11 (Spring/Summer 2016)

"Tide Lines"—*Lahar Berlin*, Vol. 1, No. 1 (December 2017)

"How my Father Became a Boat" in the online exhibition "Astonishment," at Magdalena Abakanowicz

University of the Arts, Poznan, Poland (June 2021)

"Greatest of These"—*Mobius: The Journal of Social Change*, Vol. 30, No. 1 (Spring 2019)

"Tidewater Hedge Witch" and "What I Knew"—*Oyster River Pages*, Vol. 6, No. 1 (September 2022)

"Cleaving," "Calculations from the Moral Arc," "Sleeping Porch," "How to Speak with Ghosts," "Heat Lightning," "Ship-breaking," and "Elegy with Black Holes and Hawking Radiation" in the chapbook *Heat Lightning*, Paper Nautilus Press, State College, Pennsylvania (2017)

"Consulting the book of Book of Rumination"—*River Heron Review*, Vol. 4, No. 2 (August 2021)

"Keeping the Sacraments"—*Rockvale Review*, Vol. 1, No. 4 (May 2019)

"The Benediction" and "Vessels"—*Rockvale Review*, Vol. 1, No. 11 (November 2023)

"Eye of the Storm"—*Sheila-Na-Gig* online, Vol. 5, No. 1 (Fall 2020)

"Panic Attack with Grief and Clavier"—*Subterranean Quarterly* (Fall 2013)

"Internal Combustion: A Primer"—*Susurrus: A Literary Arts Magazine of the American South*, Issue 9 (Summer 2024)

Acknowledgments

Books aren't written alone. I want to acknowledge the many people who helped realize this collection: my partner, Julia Cherry, whose patience with my need to wrest meaning from words was an act of love; Lizzie Boocock Dobkowski and Barrett Hathcock, whose yearslong encouragement sustained me; Patrick Vickers, who helped me hear the book's root chord; Lisa Mangini, who published early poems in a chapbook; Joel Brouwer, Lauren Goodwin Slaughter, Jessica Kidd, Sara Pirkle, Abraham Smith, and George Thompson, who helped me shape these pieces as a collection; my family, for understanding Faulkner's take on Keats; my oldest friend, Wade Perry, for fact-checking descriptions of our beloved bodies of water; and finally, members of International Scribblers' Union, Local #83: Rashmi Becker Grace, Marsha McSpadden, and Margaret Ann Snow—y'all make a word-Miller look good.

Title Index

After a Prolonged Illness 18
A Ripple of Hope 42
Backroads Ovid 33
Ballast 87
Bedfellows 81
Be it Ever So Humble 49
Bless Her Heart 16
Calculations from the Moral Arc 30
Cleaving 17
Consulting the Book of Rumination 46
Ebb Tide 65
Elegy for Hustle-man 54
Elegy with Black Holes and Hawking Radiation 60
Evinrude Ode 35
Eye of the Storm 44
Greatest of These 43
Heat Lightning 51
His Sky-Blue Tie 24
Hope's Hollow Bones 57

How My Father Became a Boat 25
How to Speak with Ghosts 70
Hurricane Lilies 29
Internal Combustion: A Primer 90
Keeping the Sacraments 71
Lessons in the Hidden Tongue 23
Memorial Day 59
Memories of Fort Morgan Road 80
Memory's Edges 72
My Drug of Choice Is the Dictionary 68
OED 22
Of Time and Tide 39
Panic Attack with Grief and Clavier 20
Plague Summer, College Town 48
Recipe with Healthy Crime 36
Ship-breaking 55
Sleeping Porch 34
Ten Years Gone 84
The Benediction 75
The Funeral Director's Eyes 21
The Lesson 32
The Sacrament of Solitude 74
Tidelines 89
Tidewater Hedge-Witch 61
Traffic 83
Vessels 76
What I Knew 78
What's a River? 86
What the Dead Want 64
Where Does a River End? 28
Where's Your Accent? 50

First Line Index

Above the dying mall's parking lot	65
Air sighs through bellied screens	34
All day my brother and I hear his voice	29
All our childhood's monsoon weekends	83
Another Black Belt backroad	35
Another night, golf-cart rickshaws	48
Another tidewater koan	86
A persistent sun roiled the air	64
A question strangers ask	50
A tidewater koan to soothe my mind	28
Back at the same square, my wife and I	43
Beneath the sounds	89
Do not trouble us idly	70
Each day I offer this kinetic prayer	71
Even though it's impossible	22
His flesh made word	72
I don't know what to say	18
I just called the cops on a party	51
I'm following a line of storms home	33

I never meant to stay here	49
Ingredients	36
In loss, others may turn	68
In the supermarket foyer I take a buggy	59
In those raw first days	87
It must be March again—the crows argue	84
I woke to a scream and ran	61
Jammed in his gray face	21
Like a hot shell casing	20
My brother and I rig fenders	76
My three-year-old nephew watches	25
Over a year into our slow-motion apocalypse	46
Packing list	90
pelicans plunge into tideline foam	80
So fierce, this love, in these small hours	17
Storm clouds piled high	32
Strictly speaking, there's no such thing	60
That guy from school	57
The dream is always the same	23
The new hospice nurse lacks	16
There was no handshake. No, I'm James	54
They'll have to screw his coffin shut	42
Thick, tropical winds	44
This is the Black Belt: old cotton country	30
Unlike my wont to worry every edge	75
Weeks before my brother's wedding, I mined	24
We trickle in at Christmas	39
We were brothers—wrestling	78
Whorls of rain drum the year away	74
Yesterday it was 65 and sunny	81
You died an old man's death, even though you weren't	55

www.ingramcontent.com/pod-product-compliance
Lightning Source LLC
Chambersburg PA
CBHW010724100426
42735CB00043B/3403